$Edible Gifts$

Edible Gifts

Kay Fairfax

photography by Martin Brigdale

RYLAND
PETERS
& SMALL

LONDON NEW YORK

Senior Designer Sally Powell

Commissioning Editor
Elsa Petersen-Schepelern

Production Patricia Harrington

Art Director Gabriella Le Grazie

Publishing Director Alison Starling

Food Stylist Kay Fairfax

Stylist Rebecca Duke

ISBN 1 84172 179 4

A CIP record for this book is available
from the British Library.

First published in Great Britain in 2001
by Ryland Peters & Small,
Kirkman House, 12–14 Whitfield Street,
London W1T 2RP

www.rylandpeters.com

10 9 8 7 6 5 4 3 2

Text © Kay Fairfax 2001
Design and photographs
© Ryland Peters & Small 2001

Printed and bound in China.

STERILIZATION OF PRESERVING JARS

Wash the jars in hot, soapy water and rinse in boiling
water. Place in a large saucepan and then cover with
hot water. With the lid on, bring the water to the boil
and continue boiling for 15 minutes. Turn off the heat,
then leave the jars in the hot water until just before
they are to be filled. Invert the jars onto a clean
kitchen towel to dry. Sterilize the lids for 5 minutes, by
boiling, or according to the manufacturer's instructions.
Jars should be filled and sealed while they are still hot.

The size and shape of jars are often dictated by the
type of preserve you are making. Large jars with wide
necks are needed for packing whole fruits, whereas
smaller ones, 250–500 ml, are more useful for jellies,
chutneys, conserves, etc.

Notes

All spoon measurements are level.

Ovens should be preheated to the specified temperature.
Recipes in this book were tested with a fan-assisted
oven. If using a regular oven, increase the cooking
times according to the manufacturer's instructions.

Uncooked or partly cooked eggs should not be served
to very young, old or frail people, or to pregnant women.

contents

homemade delights

There is as much joy in making and giving handmade gifts as there is in receiving them. They do not need to be extravagant and expensive – people appreciate the time and thought that has gone into the gift far more than how much it has cost.

The recipes in this book do not have any added preservatives so will not keep as long as commercial varieties, but there is no comparison between the taste of fresh, natural ingredients and those bought from the supermarket.

You won't need any special equipment for the recipes and none is too difficult or demanding, but check before you start that you have appropriate containers on hand and how long a recipe will take to mature.

Containers don't have to be new and expensive and you can package your gift with flair and originality. There are edible gifts for all ages and tastes plus instructions and creative ideas for presentation.

The old adage 'never judge a book by its cover' may still be true, but when it comes to giving and receiving, everyone loves a beautifully presented gift.

Sugar mice and coconut ice – plus chocolates and other sweets – make perfect presents. We are never too young to start learning to

chocolates, sweets & boozy fruits

cook and a foolproof recipe for the children to begin with is Coconut Ice. On the other hand we are never too old to enjoy the fruits of summer steeped in alcohol. So have fun with these recipes, but I suggest you make twice what you think you will need or you may not have anything left to give away.

9

Sugar mice are great fun – and not just for children. I made them one year for a St Patrick's Day Dinner – coloured green, they made pretty place card holders for guests to take home as a reminder of the evening.

sugar mice

500 g icing sugar, sifted

1 large egg white

1 tablespoon golden syrup

a few drops of red food colouring, enough to produce a pink mouse (optional)

decorations

silver or coloured balls for eyes

licorice strips or thin curled ribbon, for tails

Makes 10–12

Dust a work surface with a little of the icing sugar.

Put the egg white into a large bowl and whisk lightly until frothy. Add the golden syrup and stir with a wooden spoon until smooth. Add half the sifted icing sugar and, still using the wooden spoon, beat until smooth. Gradually add the remaining icing sugar and food colouring, if using, and continue beating until all the sugar has been incorporated and the mixture is smooth. You may need to add a few drops of water if the mixture is too stiff.

Transfer to the dusted work surface and knead lightly until smooth and shiny. Divide the fondant mixture into 10–12 pieces. Cover with clingfilm.

Working on one piece at a time, pinch off a small piece of fondant to make the ears and roll the remaining portion between the palms of your hand into the shape of a mouse. Divide the little piece of fondant in half and shape the 2 halves into ears. Make 2 small slits or holes in the head of the mouse and push in the ears. Carefully press silver or coloured balls into the face to make the eyes. Make a small hole for the tail, then take a thin strip of licorice or curling ribbon and push it into place.

Put the finished mice onto a flat tray lined with non-stick baking parchment. Cover with more of the parchment and let dry out completely in a warm spot for at least 2 days. Store in an airtight container for up to 6 months.

Note: Don't worry if the mice all look different, my first attempts looked more like cats than mice, some were fat and others looked half starved. Others had very lopsided ears and a very cranky expression. It was rather fun to match them to the guests!

This old favourite sweetmeat is known in Turkey itself as *rahat lokum* and means 'giving rest to the throat'. Once you have mastered the basic technique, why not experiment with your own choice of flavours such as fresh ginger with orange or cinnamon with rosewater.

turkish delight

3 tablespoons gelatine powder

400 g sugar

1 teaspoon rosewater, or to taste

2–3 drops cochineal or other red food colouring

2 teaspoons cornflour

200 g icing sugar

an 18-cm square cake tin, wetted with water

Makes about 36 pieces

Put 300 ml water in a heavy-based saucepan and bring to the boil. Reduce the heat, sprinkle in the gelatine and stir with a metal spoon until the gelatine has melted. Add the sugar and stir continuously until dissolved.

Return to the boil and continue boiling for 10 minutes. Remove from the heat and stir in the rosewater and cochineal.

Strain through a sieve lined with muslin into the prepared cake tin and let cool. Let stand overnight to set.

Next day, sift the cornflour and icing sugar into a bowl, then sprinkle a thick layer onto a work surface. Transfer the remaining cornflour-sugar mixture to a plastic bag.

Remove the Turkish Delight from the cake tin, loosening the edges if necessary with a wet knife and dipping the base of the tin into hot water for a few seconds. Turn out onto the coated work surface and cut into 3 cm squares.

Put the squares in the plastic bag, together with any sugar left on the work surface, seal the bag and shake well until they are thickly and evenly coated.

Pack into an airtight container and sprinkle over any remaining sugar mixture.

VARIATIONS

Orange Nut Delight Instead of rosewater and cochineal, add 1 tablespoon strained orange juice, 1 tablespoon orange flower water and 1 tablespoon ground crystallized orange rind at the same time as the sugar. Proceed as in the main recipe.

Lemon Nut Delight Instead of rosewater and cochineal, stir through 1 tablespoon strained lemon juice. When the mixture is beginning to set, carefully stir through 40 g blanched, chopped almonds or pistachios and proceed as in the main recipe.

This homemade recipe is much more delicious than the commercial variety – not nearly so sweet and very more-ish. It is incredibly easy to make, so no wonder it has always been a firm favourite with both children and adults.

coconut ice

750 g icing sugar, sifted, plus extra for dusting

250 ml canned sweetened condensed milk

375 g desiccated coconut

2 tablespoons freshly squeezed lemon juice

3–4 drops vanilla essence

5–6 drops cochineal or red food colouring

a baking sheet, 28 x 18 x 4 cm, lined with baking parchment and lightly dusted with sifted icing sugar

Makes about 40 pieces or 10 bars

Put the sifted icing sugar into a large bowl, add the condensed milk and mix with a wooden spoon until smooth. Add the coconut, lemon juice and vanilla and stir to form a stiff paste.

Spoon half the mixture onto the dusted baking sheet and spread evenly over the base. Level the surface.

Add the cochineal or red colouring to the remaining mixture and stir well until the mixture turns pink. Spread evenly over the white layer.

Cover and let set, then cut into 5 cm squares with a small, sharp knife and package in clear cellophane bags. Alternatively, cut in half crossways across the rectangle, then in 5 strips lengthways, giving 10 bars. Wrap the bars individually in clear cellophane paper.

Coconut Ice will keep in an airtight container for about 2 weeks.

Note: When making chocolates, always buy the best brand of chocolate available and grate or break it into small pieces before melting.

Chocolate should never come into contact with direct heat or water, so if possible use a double boiler. Excess heat, or even a drop of moisture will cause the chocolate to 'seize' – become grainy – burn or turn bitter, and there is no way to retrieve the mess.

Chocolate can also be melted in the microwave: consult the handbook before you start, use the lowest setting and stir and check about every 60 seconds.

Truffles are supposed to look like the rare and elusive fungi of the same name – they are a traditional Christmas speciality in France. Homemade truffles have a much lighter, fresher taste than the commercial varieties and, if you hide them, will last several weeks in an airtight container in the refrigerator.

chocolate truffles

300 ml double cream

500 g couverture chocolate or dark cooking chocolate, grated

150 g cocoa powder, sifted

Makes about 50

Pour the cream into a heavy-based saucepan or double boiler and bring to the boil. Remove the pan from the heat and let cool until lukewarm. Add the grated chocolate and beat with an electric mixer for about 5 minutes. Set aside to cool, then beat for a further 5 minutes. Transfer the bowl to the refrigerator and chill for at least 10 minutes or until the mixture is firm enough to shape with your hands.

Sift the cocoa into a deep bowl or spread a thick layer on a baking sheet. Make sure your hands are clean and dry, then dust them with cocoa and, using about 2 heaped teaspoons of the mixture, quickly shape into a ball and roll in the cocoa. Put in little paper cases and store in airtight containers.

Coconut and Vanilla Truffles Add 45–90 g desiccated coconut and 1 tablespoon vanilla essence. Shape the mixture into small balls. Dip each one into 750 g melted chocolate and roll in cocoa as in the main recipe.

Rum-and-Raisin Truffles Add 2 tablespoons of rum and 80–160 g seedless raisins. Shape the mixture into small balls and roll each one in chocolate threads or sprinkles, about 125 g.

Coffee and Nut Truffles Add 2–3 tablespoons instant coffee granules to the hot cream, stir until dissolved and proceed as in the main recipe. Pipe the mixture into small paper or foil confectionery cases and sprinkle with finely chopped nuts, about 150 g.

Boozy berries taste as good as they look. Any combination of summer berries can be used, including black, red or white currants, blackberries, blueberries, raspberries, boysenberries and small strawberries. They make an unexpectedly colourful pudding in winter, served with whipped cream or crème fraîche, and are excellent used as an accompaniment to roast duck, chicken or game. Best of all, you can drink the juice separately as a liqueur.

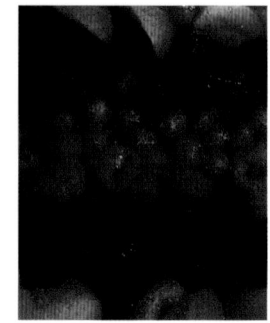

summer fruits in cointreau

1 kg berry fruits (a mixture of berries such as small strawberries, blueberries, raspberries and others)

375 g caster sugar

450 ml Cointreau

a 1.5 litre preserving jar, sterilized

Makes 1.5 litres

Wash, drain and pat the berries dry with kitchen paper. Remove all leaves, stalks or damaged pieces.

Arrange in layers about 3 cm deep in the sterilized glass jar, adding about 3 tablespoons sugar between each layer until the jar is full.

Pour in enough Cointreau to cover the fruit and fill the jar completely. Seal, label and date and store in a cool, dark place for several months before using. Rotate the jar several times during storage to help the sugar dissolve.

Always choose figs of similar size: they must be firm and not over-ripe, otherwise when you prick them juice may seep out and discolour the liquid. You may prefer to use two smaller jars instead of one large one for a special gift.

figs in muscat

1–1½ kg firm, ripe figs, about 12–15

125 g sugar

300 ml Muscat or port

1.5 litre preserving jar, sterilized

Makes 1.5 litres

Wipe the figs with a damp cloth and pat dry with kitchen paper. Trim the stalks and carefully prick the skins 5–6 times with a sterilized needle or cocktail stick.

Put the sugar and 250 ml water in a saucepan and stir over a low heat until the sugar is completely dissolved. Set aside to cool and stir in the Muscat or port. Carefully pack the figs into the prepared jar, without damaging the fruit, then pour in Muscat to cover the fruit and fill the jar completely. Seal, label and date.

Store in a dark, cool place for several weeks before using.

The very small variety of pears, perfect for this recipe, are sometimes called Lebanese Pears, but if you have trouble finding them you can always use larger ones. If using a larger variety, peel, quarter, core and remove pips and follow the recipe below.

tipsy pears

500 g small, firm ripe pears

300 ml red Burgundy

200 g sugar

1 cinnamon stick

125 ml brandy

750 ml preserving jar, sterilized

Makes about 750 ml

Carefully wash and dry the pears, making sure the stalks are still attached. Put the Burgundy and sugar in a preserving pan or large saucepan and stir over a low heat until the sugar has completely dissolved.

Add the prepared pears and cinnamon stick to the syrup and bring to the boil. Reduce the heat and simmer until the pears are just tender, about 5 minutes. Remove the cinnamon stick and, using a slotted spoon, pack the pears into the prepared jar.

Return the syrup to the boil and boil rapidly without stirring for 5 minutes. Strain the syrup and add enough brandy to make 625–750 ml of liquid, or enough to cover the pears completely.

Pour the syrup over the pears and top up the jars with more brandy if necessary. Seal, label and date.

Store in a dark, cool place for at least 2 months before using.

All the recipes chosen for this section can be made a few days ahead and will still be fresh enough to give away – they are all easy to

cakes & biscuits

package and transport. Why not try the Chinese fortune cookies for a children's party with appropriate jokes or, for your next dinner party, with fun messages in each one for the guests to read out?

21

Fortune cookies are not only delicious to eat but are great fun to make and to give to friends, especially at Christmas and New Year. The whole family can be involved making up jokes and fortunes or, if inspiration fails, you can buy great little books of funny quotes and sayings instead.

chinese fortune cookies

100 g plain flour

2 teaspoons ground ginger

3 large egg whites

100 g icing sugar, sifted

115 g unsalted butter, melted

a 6 cm biscuit cutter or glass

3–4 baking sheets, greased and lightly floured

Makes about 18–20

Sift the flour and ginger into a small bowl. Put the egg whites into a large bowl and whisk until just frothy. Add the icing sugar and melted butter and whisk until the mixture is smooth.

Beat in the flour and ginger mixture until the mixture forms a smooth paste, then set aside to rest for 15–20 minutes.

Using a biscuit cutter or the top of a glass, gently mark 6 circles about 6 cm in diameter on each baking sheet. Working on one sheet at a time, put a heaped teaspoon of a mixture in the centre of each circle. Smooth with a flat knife to fill each circle.

Bake in a preheated oven at 180°C (350°F) Gas 4 for 6–7 minutes or until the edges start to brown. Remove the sheet from the oven and carefully and quickly slide each cookie onto a flat surface. Put a message in the centre of each cookie and fold the cookie in half, then fold the 2 points together – the dough is very pliable while hot.

Continue baking and filling each cookie as they are ready – unless you have lots of helpers, you can only work on one sheet at a time, or the cookies will dry out before they can be folded.

Cool on a wire rack until completely dry. If packing in boxes to give as a gift, wrap in tissue paper first, so they won't break.

These little French cakes are delicious served for breakfast, afternoon tea or with coffee after dinner. They are also perfect for using up leftover egg whites or frozen ones left over from an earlier recipe. Remember that if you are using frozen egg whites, they must be thawed to room temperature because chilled egg whites will not beat.

friands

180 g unsalted butter

225 g icing sugar, sifted, plus extra for dusting

5 tablespoons plain flour

90 g ground almonds

5 egg whites

1 tablespoon finely grated lemon or orange zest

12 small oval barquettes or dariole moulds or mini loaf or muffin tins

a baking sheet

Makes 12

Put the butter in a small saucepan and melt over a very low heat. Let cool. Brush the barquettes, moulds or tins with melted butter.

Sift the flour and icing sugar together into a large bowl. Using a wooden spoon, stir in the ground almonds. Put the egg whites into a separate bowl and whisk gently until light and frothy. Fold them through the dry ingredients.

Pour in the remaining melted butter and stir well. Stir in the lemon or orange zest.

Put the greased moulds on a baking sheet and fill each one three-quarters full with the mixture. Put the sheet onto the middle shelf of a preheated oven and bake at 200°C (400°F) Gas 6 for 10 minutes, then turn them on the sheet and bake for a further 7–10 minutes. They should be golden on top and firm to touch in the centre.

Remove the sheet from the oven and let stand for about 5 minutes. Carefully invert each one onto a wire rack. When cool, dust generously with sifted icing sugar, then store in an airtight container. Friands taste even better the next day and will last for at least 3 days stored this way.

Gingerbread with a difference. This is a delicious family favourite even without the icing and with chocolate fudge icing on top it makes a special gift. You can leave it whole as a large cake or cut into squares to be served as an after dinner treat.

chocolate gingerbread

200 g muscovado sugar

100 g unsalted butter

250 g golden syrup

400 g plain flour

1½ teaspoons baking powder

½ teaspoon bicarbonate soda

2½ teaspoons ground ginger

1 egg, lightly beaten

150 ml full fat milk

chocolate fudge icing

150 g icing sugar, sifted

3–4 tablespoons cocoa powder, sifted

50 g unsalted butter, softened

100 g finely chopped nuts (optional)

a 23 cm square cake tin, greased and lined

Makes about 16

Put the sugar, butter and golden syrup into a large saucepan. Heat gently over a low heat, stirring continuously, until the sugar has dissolved completely. Set aside to cool.

Sift the flour, baking powder, bicarbonate of soda and ground ginger into a bowl. Pour the cooled syrup over the dry ingredients and add the egg and milk. Stir until smooth.

Pour the mixture into the prepared cake tin and bake in a preheated oven at 150°C (300°F) Gas 2 for 1¼–1½ hours, or until a skewer inserted in the centre of the cake comes out clean. Let cool in the tin.

To make the icing, put the icing sugar, cocoa and softened butter in a bowl and mix well. Gradually add a little hot water, 1 tablespoon at a time, mixing well, until the icing is of a spreadable consistency. Spread the icing evenly over the top of the cake and swirl gently with a fork. Sprinkle with chopped nuts if using and, when the icing has set, cut into 6 cm squares.

The original American brownie, with its unusual rich, gooey texture, is a chocoholic's dream come true. You can add the chopped nuts to the mixture or sprinkle them over the icing – either way is equally delicious.

chocolate brownies

170 g unsalted butter

3 eggs

325 g caster sugar

75 g cocoa powder, sifted, plus extra for dusting

½ teaspoon vanilla essence

75 g plain flour, sifted

250 g dark chocolate, finely chopped or grated

150 g nuts, such as walnuts, almonds or pecan nuts, coarsely chopped (optional)

chocolate cream

100 ml double cream

125 g finely chopped or grated dark chocolate

a cake tin, 28 x 18 x 1 cm, lined with baking parchment extending 5 cm beyond the long ends

Makes about 15

Put the butter in a small saucepan and melt it slowly over a low heat.

Put the eggs in a bowl, whisk lightly, then whisk in the sugar. Stir in the melted butter, the cocoa and vanilla. Using a wooden spoon or spatula, stir in the flour. Stir through the chopped chocolate and the nuts, if using.

Pour into the prepared cake tin and bake in a preheated oven at 160°C (325°F) Gas 3 for 25–30 minutes or until just firm in the centre and still moist at the bottom.

Remove from the oven and let stand, still in the tin, on a wire rack until completely cool.

Using the overhanging paper at the ends, carefully lift the brownie onto a flat board and peel off the paper. Dust with sifted cocoa or, for serious chocolate lovers, cover with chocolate cream and sprinkle with finely chopped nuts, if using. Cut into 6 cm squares.

Do not overcook brownies, they are not meant to have the consistency of a cake and should be moist and gooey in the middle. They will dry out as they cool.

Chocolate Cream

Put the cream in a saucepan and heat until just simmering. Add the chocolate and stir until smooth and glossy. Transfer to the refrigerator for about 1 hour until the cream is firm enough to spread over the brownies.

How long do curds last? There's no need to worry, because once your

curds, butters & conserves

family has tasted them, you'll be lucky if there are any left to give away. The jellies are so good you probably won't want to part with them either – even to your best friends. You don't need large amounts of these recipes, so keep small decorative jars to use and don't forget to sterilize them carefully before filling.

Hide this brandy butter as soon as you've made it or there'll be none left for Christmas Day – and definitely none for Boxing Day. It makes a fabulous present when accompanied by a box of homemade mini Christmas puddings or mince pies. The orange juice and grated zest mean that it's not as sweet as the usual brandy butter, and it's good enough to eat by the spoonful without the pudding or the mince pies. You can make a separate batch for the children, leaving out the brandy. If you want a larger amount, just double the recipe.

orange brandy butter

250 g unsalted butter, softened

250 g icing sugar, sifted

4 tablespoons ground almonds

finely grated zest of 1 orange and 1 tablespoon strained freshly squeezed orange juice

1–2 tablespoons brandy

Makes about 1 litre, or 525 g

Put the butter and icing sugar in a large bowl and beat until light and creamy. Add the ground almonds and beat again. Stir in the grated orange zest and strained juice, then the brandy. Mix well.

The brandy butter will keep for several weeks in an airtight container in the refrigerator. It is very rich so it is better to package it in several small containers rather than one large one, unless it is for the family for Christmas.

Note: To prevent pure icing sugar from going lumpy, keep it sealed in the refrigerator and sift as required. Pure icing sugar is pulverized white sugar, as distinct from soft icing sugar, to which starch has been added to prevent it from clumping. Soft icing sugar is not suitable for most icing purposes.

A jelly that tastes as good as it looks – worth having in the store cupboard all year round. A traditional accompaniment for turkey, it is also good with roast lamb.

cranberry jelly

2 kg cranberries, fresh or frozen*

warmed sugar (see recipe)

a preserving pan

jelly bag or colander lined with 2 layers of muslin

3 preserving jars, 250 ml each, sterilized (see page 4)

Makes 750 ml

*Black or redcurrants may be used instead of the cranberries.

Wash and drain the berries. Put in a preserving pan or large saucepan with 1 litre water, bring to the boil and simmer until soft, about 30 minutes. Mash them occasionally. Arrange a jelly bag or colander lined with a double layer of muslin over a deep, non-metal container. Fill with the cranberry mixture and let the liquid drip through for several hours or overnight. Never be tempted to squeeze or stir the bag to hurry the process, or your jelly will be cloudy.

Next day, measure the liquid, then measure 500 ml sugar for every 500 ml of the liquid. Pour the liquid into a preserving pan. Bring slowly to the boil. Stir until the sugar has dissolved. Boil rapidly until setting point is reached, about 10 minutes (see page 38). Skim and pour into hot sterilized jars. Seal while hot. Label and date.

The jelly will keep for 6 months and should be refrigerated after opening.

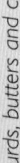

A decorative and delicious jelly, very good with pork – once your friends taste it, they will be queueing up for the recipe.

apple, mint and peppercorn jelly

1 kg green cooking apples, unpeeled

1 unwaxed lemon

a small bunch of mint, plus 2 tablespoons chopped mint

100 ml white wine vinegar

warmed sugar (see recipe)

2 tablespoons bottled green peppercorns, drained

a preserving pan

jelly bag or colander lined with 2 layers of muslin

2 preserving jars, 250 ml each, sterilized (see page 4)

Makes 625 ml

Wash the apples and chop into quarters. Wash the lemon and cut in half. Wash the mint thoroughly and shake off any excess water. Put the apples, lemon, bunch of mint and vinegar in a preserving pan and add 500 ml water.

Bring to the boil, then reduce to a simmer and cook for 1 hour until the apples are soft – mash them occasionally with the back of a wooden spoon to help them break down. Arrange a jelly bag or a colander lined with a double layer of muslin over a deep, non-metal container. Fill with the apple mixture and let the liquid drip through for several hours or overnight. Never be tempted to squeeze or stir the bag to hurry the process, or your jelly will be cloudy.

Next day, measure the liquid, then measure 500 ml sugar for every 500 ml of the liquid. Pour the liquid into a preserving pan. Bring slowly to the boil. Stir until the sugar has dissolved, then add the chopped mint and boil rapidly for 10 minutes or until setting point is reached (see page 38).

Bruise the peppercorns lightly and stir into the jelly. Let cool, stirring occasionally to make sure the mint and peppercorns are evenly distributed. Pour into hot, sterilized jars. Seal, label and date.

The jelly will keep for 6 months, and should be refrigerated after opening.

Curd makes an extra special gift if you also include a packet of small meringues or mini pastry cases. This may taste a little sweet when first made, but it will lose sweetness once it is cold. Also, it is well worth taking the time to strain the beaten eggs as there is often a surprising amount of residue left in the strainer.

grapefruit and lime curd

1 unwaxed grapefruit

2 unwaxed limes

4 large eggs

275 g caster sugar

3 preserving jars, 250 ml each, sterilized

Makes about 750 ml

Wash and dry the fruit. Finely grate the zest of the grapefruit and 1 of the limes. Squeeze the juice, strain and measure 4 tablespoons lime juice and 125 ml grapefruit juice.

Put the eggs in a bowl and whisk them lightly. Put the strained juices, grated zest and sugar in the top of a double boiler, or a heatproof bowl set over a saucepan of simmering water. Stir.

Strain the beaten eggs into the mixture and stir over a very low heat until the sugar has dissolved and the mixture begins to thicken. Continue stirring until the mixture is thick enough to coat the back of a wooden spoon, about 20–40 minutes.

Pour the curd into hot, sterilized, dry jars. Cover, seal, label and date. If unopened, this curd will keep for up to 8 weeks in the refrigerator. Use within 10–14 days of opening.

A slightly richer and more creamy curd than the grapefruit recipe because it also includes butter. When filling glass containers with hot liquid always stand the warm jars on a damp cloth. This not only helps to stop them slipping but will also make sure they won't break.

lemon or lime curd

4 unwaxed limes or 2 large unwaxed lemons

4 large eggs

225 g caster sugar

125 g soft, unsalted butter

3 preserving jars, 250 ml each, sterilized

Makes about 750 ml

Wash and dry the limes or lemons. Finely grate the zest and squeeze and strain the juice. Measure out 125 ml juice and 1 tablespoon grated zest.

Put the eggs in a bowl and whisk lightly.

Put the measured juice and zest, sugar and butter in the top of a double boiler, or a heatproof bowl set over a saucepan of simmering water. Stir until the sugar has dissolved and the butter melted.

Strain the beaten eggs into the mixture and stir well. Continue to stir until the curd is thick enough to coat the back of a wooden spoon, at least 10 minutes, but up to 30 minutes.

Pour into hot, sterilized, dry jars. Cover, seal, label and date.

This curd will keep, unopened, for up to 8 weeks in the refrigerator. It is delicious as a spread on toast or in sandwiches, and for filling pies or cakes.

Take a day out with the family or friends and pick your own fresh fruit to make this jam. It's a fun way to spend a day and local or home-grown strawberries have so much more flavour and aroma than the commercial varieties.

strawberry jam

2 kg strawberries

2 kg sugar

juice of 4 lemons

1 teaspoon butter

olive oil, for greasing

a preserving pan

4 preserving jars, 500 ml each, sterilized

Makes about 2 litres

Wash the strawberries, pat dry with kitchen paper, then hull them. Grease a preserving pan lightly with olive oil. Add the fruit, sugar and lemon juice, stir well, then let stand for several hours until juices form.

Gradually bring to the boil stirring gently until the sugar has dissolved (about 10 minutes). Add the butter and boil until setting point is reached, about 2–5 minutes (see note below). Remove from the heat and skim the surface with a slotted spoon or fine strainer. Pour into hot, dry, sterilized jars. Seal, label and date.

Setting Point: To test jams for setting, remove the pan from the heat. Take a small spoonful of the jam and put on a chilled plate. Let cool. Push it with your fingertip – if the jam is ready, the surface will set and wrinkle. If using a sugar thermometer, warm it before putting it into hot jam. A good set should be assured when the temperature reaches 100°C (220°F). When setting point is reached, remove immediately from the heat because overboiling causes darkening and affects the consistency of the jam.

Although you can now buy cherries out of season, for this recipe, wait until local cherries are in abundance – they will be of better quality and more reasonably priced.

cherry and orange jam

1 kg pitted cherries, weighed after pitting, pits reserved

grated zest, freshly squeezed juice and pips of 1 large orange, about 200 ml

freshly squeezed juice of 1 large lemon, about 75 ml

1 kg sugar

1 tablespoon slivered almonds

1 tablespoon Cointreau or Grand Marnier

a small muslin bag

a preserving pan

3 preserving jars, 500 ml each, sterilized

Makes 1.5 litres

Put the cherry pits and orange pips in the muslin bag and tie securely.

Put the fruit, zest, juices and muslin bag in a preserving pan or large saucepan. Simmer over a low heat until the cherries are soft. While the cherries are cooking, put the sugar in a baking tin in a preheated oven at 150°C (300°F) Gas 2 for about 10–15 minutes to heat through.

Remove the muslin bag from the pan and slowly add the warm sugar. When the sugar has dissolved, turn up the heat and boil rapidly until setting point is reached (see note page 38). Check after 10 minutes as this jam very quickly turns to treacle. Remove the pan from the heat and carefully stir through the Cointreau and slivered almonds. Let cool slightly before bottling into hot sterilized jars. (If bottled while still hot the cherries and almonds will all rise to the surface.) Seal, label and date.

These flavoured oils, scented with aromatic whole spices, chillies and fresh herbs, will be a welcome addition to even the most

vinegars, oils & olives

sophisticated cook's kitchen. Their looks belie how easy and inexpensive they are to make, but always use a good quality oil, preferably an extra virgin olive oil and not a bland non-specific vegetable variety. The same advice applies to the herbed olives: they must have good quality oil to bring out the best flavour.

Note: Sterilize attractively shaped jars or bottles which seal tightly and make sure the vinegar reaches the top of the bottle. Always let the vinegar cool completely before sealing.

If a cork is too large for the container, cut a wedge-shaped piece out of the end. The gap will close when pushed in.

Raspberry vinegar was indispensable in the Victorian pantry and is now in favour again. Flavoured vinegars are perfect for deglazing the juices of roasted poultry, veal or pork dishes. They also make a most refreshing summer drink – put 1 tablespoon in a glass with ice cubes and fill with soda water. A jigger of brandy makes them even more refreshing!

berry vinegar

500 g–1 kg raspberries, blackberries or blueberries

1 litre white wine vinegar

sugar (see method)

2 bottles, 500 ml each, sterilized

Makes 1 litre

Pick over the berries carefully, then put into a large jar or ceramic basin. Cover with the vinegar and let stand in a cool place for 7–10 days. Keep covered and stir gently every day.

After 10 days, strain through a fine nylon sieve or muslin. Let drip but do not squeeze the fruit. Measure the vinegar, then measure 625 ml sugar for every 500 ml liquid. Bring the vinegar gently to the boil, add the sugar and simmer for 10 minutes. Skim if necessary. Let cool. Bottle and seal tightly before storing in a cool place.

lemon spice vinegar

625 ml white wine vinegar

a small cinnamon stick, about 7 cm

2 small fresh bay leaves

zest of 1 lemon, removed in a long spiral

long spiral of fresh or dried orange zest the same size as the lemon

1 teaspoon black peppercorns

3 cloves

2–3 sprigs of lemon thyme

½ teaspoon coriander seeds

1 bottle, 650 ml, with screw-top, stopper or cork, sterilized

1 funnel

Makes 650 ml

Put the vinegar in a saucepan and heat gently over a low heat. Add all the remaining ingredients and let steep in the pan until cool. Carefully poke the herbs and spices into the bottle and, using a funnel, pour in the vinegar.

Seal with a tight-fitting screw-top lid, stopper or cork.

Place the bottle in a warm sunny position for 2–3 weeks to draw out the flavours. When the flavour is fully developed, remove the solids, strain and rebottle. Store the vinegar in a cool dark place, then add fresh rind and a sprig of lemon thyme before giving as a gift.

vinegars, oils and olives

43

Flavoured vinegars are usually made from white wine or cider vinegar – and occasionally red wine or sherry vinegar. Always use a good quality variety with an acetic acid content of at least 5 per cent and remember to leave enough time for the vinegar to stand for several weeks to mature before it will be ready to give away.

spicy mint vinegar

500 ml white wine vinegar

4 sprigs of fresh mint, 10–12 cm each

1 fresh bay leaf

½ teaspoon black peppercorns

3 dried red chillies

1 bottle, 500 ml, sterilized

Makes 500 ml

Put the vinegar in a stainless steel saucepan and warm over a low heat. Wash and dry the mint and bay leaf and coarsely crush the peppercorns. Put them into the prepared bottle, then add the chillies. Using a funnel, fill the bottle with the warmed vinegar. Let cool before sealing with a screw-top lid, stopper or cork.

Put the bottle in a warm sunny position for 2–3 weeks to draw out the flavours. When the flavour is fully developed, remove the solids, strain and rebottle. Store the vinegar in a cool dark place.

When giving it as a gift, add a fresh sprig of mint.

Flavoured vinegar is ideal to use in salad dressings and this version will add a special piquancy to sauces, soups and casseroles. It is also particularly good to add to marinades and to deglaze pans after cooking meat, fish and poultry.

chilli vinegar

500 ml white or red wine vinegar

2–3 fresh bay leaves

4–6 small red chillies, fresh or dried

1 bottle, 500 ml, sterilized

Makes 500 ml

Put the vinegar in a stainless steel saucepan and warm over a low heat. Wash and dry the bay leaves and fresh chillies.

Put the bay leaves, chillies and garlic in the prepared bottle and fill with the warmed vinegar. Let cool before sealing with a tight fitting screw-top lid, stopper or cork.

Proceed as for Spicy Mint Vinegar, adding a fresh chilli and fresh bay leaf to give as a gift.

This is a delightful piquant oil and is the perfect partner for a green summer salad and wonderful for basting roast duck.

orange and saffron oil

5–7 long thin strips of fresh or dried orange peel

½–1 teaspoon saffron threads

1 teaspoon coriander seeds, bruised

a sprig of rosemary, about 12 cm

olive oil

1 bottle, about 500–600 ml, sterilized

Makes 500–600 ml

Put the orange peel, saffron, coriander seeds and rosemary sprig into a prepared glass bottle. Using a funnel, add enough oil to fill the bottle.

Seal tightly and store in a cool dark place for 2 weeks before using.

A very useful oil to keep in the store cupboard: try stirring a few tablespoons through hot pasta with a handful of freshly chopped herbs and grated Parmesan cheese – or use it in the wok with your next stir-fry.

chilli oil

3 fresh bay leaves

6 fresh small red chillies

1 teaspoon whole black peppercorns

olive oil

1 bottle, about 500–600 ml, sterilized

Makes 500–600 ml

Wash and dry the bay leaves and chillies. Put all the ingredients in the prepared glass bottle and, using a funnel, fill the bottle with olive oil. Remember to leave enough room at the top if you are using a cork or stopper instead of a screw-top lid.

Store in a cool dark place for at least 2 weeks before using.

Herbs should be picked early in the morning before the sun vaporizes their oils: always choose fresh young growth that hasn't yet flowered, as the flavour is more intense. The sprigs should be about 15 cm long.

green herb oil

a sprig of tarragon

a sprig of rosemary

a sprig of sage

a sprig of thyme

3 small fresh bay leaves

1 teaspoon whole black or red peppercorns

olive oil

1 bottle, about 500–600 ml, sterilized

Makes 500–600 ml

Wash and dry the herbs and push them into a prepared glass bottle. Add the peppercorns. Using a funnel, fill the bottle with olive oil and seal with a tightly fitting non-corrosive screw-top lid, stopper or cork.

Store in a cool dark place for at least 1 week before using.

Note: Oils do not last forever and those containing fresh herbs are best used within 3 months of making. The ingredients for the oil recipes on these 2 pages are enough to fill a bottle of 500–600 ml capacity, but try using 2 smaller bottles so that they will be used up more quickly.

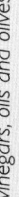

vinegars, oils and olives

The flavourful marinating oil from these olives is delicious – use it separately in cooking or on salads. You can top up the oil and the olives as they are used.

balsamic and oregano olives

500 g black or green olives

6 tablespoons olive oil

2 tablespoons balsamic vinegar

1 fat garlic clove, chopped

1 teaspoon chopped oregano

a wide-necked glass jar with a non-metallic lid,
about 600 ml, sterilized

Makes about 600 ml

Rinse the olives and leave to drain on kitchen paper.

Put all the ingredients into the sterilized jar and seal. Gently shake or turn the jar upside down a few times to coat the olives.

Let stand in a cool place for a least 2 days before serving, then use within 1 month.

Once opened, keep stored in the refrigerator and remember to remove 30 minutes before serving.

According to your choice of herbs, these olives could have an interesting effect if eaten in great quantities: coriander, for instance, was used in the Middle Ages as an aphrodisiac and thyme was taken as part of a ritual to enable one to see fairies.

green olives with coriander and thyme

500 g green olives, rinsed and drained

1 teaspoon black peppercorns, crushed

1 fat garlic clove, finely chopped, not crushed

3–4 small strips of lemon peel

4 tablespoons finely chopped fresh coriander and thyme leaves

olive oil, to cover

2 wide-necked glass preserving jars, 300 ml each, sterilized

Makes 600 ml

Put all the ingredients, except the oil, in the jars.

Fill the jars with the oil until all the olives are covered. Shake gently to mix.

Store in a cool place and let marinate for 1 week or 10 days, then use within 1 month.

Most fresh herbs can be used in this recipe, but the basic varieties are thyme and parsley. Don't use basil as it can turn black in oil.

stuffed olives with fresh herbs

3 tablespoons olive oil

4 tablespoons finely chopped fresh herbs

1 large garlic clove, finely chopped, not crushed

1 teaspoon black peppercorns, crushed

3–4 small strips of fresh lemon zest

250 g stuffed green olives, rinsed and drained

1 preserving jar, about 300 ml, sterilized

Makes about 300 ml

Put the oil, herbs, garlic, peppercorns and lemon zest into a bowl and mix well. Add the olives and stir gently until they are all well coated with oil.

Transfer to the prepared jar, seal and store in the refrigerator. Shake the jar occasionally to move the olives around.

They can be eaten after 24 hours and will keep for about 1 month.

chutneys, relishes & mustards

These are much loved, classic gifts that everyone enjoys. Such is the variety of ingredients for chutneys, relishes and mustards, that they can be made all year round and will keep for ages. When making a batch always hide a few extra jars in your store cupboard and you will never be caught short for want of a small gift for that unexpected occasion.

It is impossible to give exact quantities for many of these recipes, as it depends on how juicy your fruit and vegetables are and exactly what size jars you have. This relish is not only decorative, but it will also enhance any roasted meat, poultry or game dishes.

red pepper relish

2 cucumbers, about 20 cm each, peeled, deseeded and diced

4 onions, 2 red and 2 white, sliced

4 celery stalks, chopped

2 large garlic cloves, finely crushed (optional)

2 large red peppers, deseeded and finely chopped

2 large green peppers, deseeded and finely chopped

5 tablespoons sea salt

400 ml cider or white wine vinegar

1 teaspoon mustard seeds

300 g caster sugar

½ teaspoon ground allspice

½ teaspoon fennel seeds

2 preserving jars, 300 ml each, sterilized

Makes 600 ml

Put all the vegetables into large bowl, sprinkle with the salt, cover and refrigerate overnight.

Next day, drain, pressing to get rid of the liquid. Put into a plastic sieve and rinse with cold running water. Drain again, then press with kitchen paper to dry off as much as possible. Set aside.

Put all the remaining ingredients into a saucepan and bring to the boil. Add the drained vegetables and return to the boil. Simmer for 30 minutes or until the vegetables are just tender.

Spoon the mixture into the prepared jars. Seal tightly, label and date.

Store for 3 months before eating. After opening, keep the jars covered in the refrigerator and use the relish within 2–3 weeks.

A relish with a delicious tropical flavour – don't be afraid to try different combinations. Use other fruits if you can't find tropical varieties, and maybe add a few raisins.

summer fruit relish

I small ripe mango, peeled and chopped fairly small

I small papaya, peeled and chopped fairly small

2 onions, peeled and finely sliced

185 g dates, pitted and chopped

2 large guavas, peeled and chopped fairly small, or the pulp and seeds of 6 passionfruit

2 medium cooking apples, peeled, cored and chopped

2 fresh apricots, pitted and chopped

375 ml white wine vinegar or cider vinegar

375 g sugar

2 tablespoons sea salt

I cm fresh ginger, peeled and grated

6 juniper berries, slightly crushed, or I teaspoon powdered allspice

I heaped tablespoon freshly ground black pepper

a preserving pan

2 preserving jars, 600 ml each, sterilized

Makes 1.25 litres

Put all the ingredients into a preserving pan or large, heavy-based saucepan. Heat slowly, stirring until the sugar has dissolved. Bring to the boil and simmer for about I hour 40 minutes or until very thick. Spoon into hot sterilized jars and cover with plastic-coated lids. Keep for 3 months before opening. After opening, keep covered in the refrigerator and use within 2–3 weeks.

chutneys, relishes and mustards

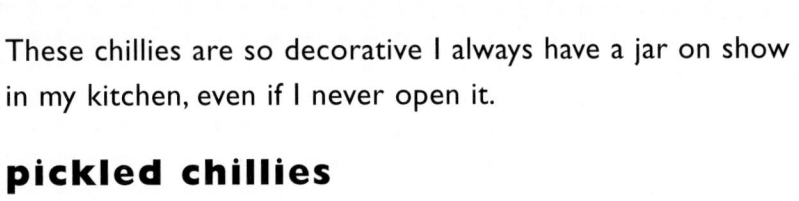

These chillies are so decorative I always have a jar on show in my kitchen, even if I never open it.

pickled chillies

about 750 g red serrano chillies, about 5 cm long

250 ml white wine vinegar

200 g caster sugar

½ teaspoon sea salt

2 preserving jars, 500 ml each, sterilized

Makes about 1 litre

Thoroughly wash and drain the chillies. Leave them whole or halve them lengthways and remove the seeds if you prefer.

Put them in a saucepan with the vinegar, sugar and salt. Bring to the boil and let simmer until the sugar has dissolved and the chillies are tender, about 6–8 minutes.

Remove from the heat and let cool before packing into the sterilized jars. Seal tightly, label and date, then store in the refrigerator. Leave for 2 weeks before using. After opening, keep covered in the refrigerator and use within 2–3 weeks.

Note: When handling chillies, wear gloves, or use tongs or a knife and fork, and keep your hands well away from your eyes.

The perfect gift for friends who enjoy hot and spicy flavours.

preserved sweet chillies

125 g medium to large fresh red chillies

440 g sugar

450 ml white wine vinegar

2 preserving jars, 200 ml each, sterilized

Makes 425 ml

Slice the chillies crossways into 2 cm pieces. Rinse well and drain, removing as many seeds as possible for a less fiery flavour. Put the chillies and sugar into a heavy-based saucepan and add the vinegar. Bring slowly to the boil, then let simmer until the chillies are tender, about 5–7 minutes. Remove from the heat then set aside to cool. Spoon into the prepared jars, seal tightly, label and date.

Store in a cool, dark place for 2 weeks before using. After opening, keep covered in the refrigerator and use within 2–3 weeks.

chutneys, relishes and mustards

55

A special homemade gift for Christmas or Thanksgiving, this chutney can be made at least a month in advance and, being a cooked variety, it will keep for several months if stored in a cool, dark, dry place. It is very colourful and decorative and is the perfect accompaniment for Christmas turkey and ham, hot or cold poultry, salads and cheese. Try your hand at making your own labels – they are very easy to create on a computer and lend that extra personal touch to the gift.

cranberry and raisin chutney

500 g fresh or frozen cranberries

125 ml white wine vinegar or cider vinegar

90 g seedless raisins

60 g chopped nuts (Brazil nuts or almonds are best)

finely grated zest and juice of 2 lemons

½ teaspoon ground ginger

½ teaspoon paprika

½ teaspoon ground cinnamon

½ teaspoon sea salt

375 g sugar

a preserving pan

4 preserving jars, 250 ml each, sterilized

Makes 1 litre

Put all the ingredients, except the cranberries, into a preserving pan or heavy-based stainless steel saucepan. Add 175 ml water, bring to the boil, reduce the heat and simmer until tender. Add the cranberries and simmer for 40 minutes or until the fruit is soft but not disintegrated, about 45 minutes.

Spoon into the prepared jars. Cover and seal tightly, label and date. Store in a cool dark place for 2–3 weeks before using. After opening, keep covered in the refrigerator and use within 2 months.

chutneys, relishes and mustards

Delicious with hot or cold roast pork, lamb, grilled fish and curries.

gingered banana chutney

500 g onions, coarsely chopped

375 g dates, coarsely chopped

2 garlic cloves, coarsely chopped

750 g bananas, weighed after peeling

375 ml malt vinegar

250 g seedless raisins

125 g fresh ginger, peeled and finely chopped

250 ml pineapple juice

juice of 2 lemons, about 125 ml

1 tablespoon mustard seeds

1 teaspoon sea salt

3 whole cloves

Tabasco sauce, to taste

3 preserving jars, 250 ml each, sterilized

Makes 750 ml

Put the onions, dates and garlic in a heavy-based stainless steel saucepan. Add the mashed bananas and vinegar. Bring to the boil, cover and simmer for about 20 minutes.

Add the raisins, ginger, fruit juices and spices. Bring to the boil and simmer for 10–15 minutes, stirring constantly until the mixture is thick. Add Tabasco to taste. Pour into hot, sterilized jars. Cool, seal, label and date.

Store in the refrigerator for 2 days before using. Most chutneys improve by storing for 2–3 weeks before using: this one can be eaten after 2–3 days. After opening, keep covered in the refrigerator and use within 2 months.

Perfect to serve with hot or cold poultry, salads or a mature Cheddar cheese.

peach chutney

1 onion, chopped, about 60 g

500 g seedless raisins, chopped

1 garlic clove, chopped

2 kg peaches, peeled, pitted and diced

125 g fresh ginger, peeled and chopped

2 tablespoons chilli powder

2 tablespoons mustard seeds

1 tablespoon sea salt

1 litre cider vinegar

800 g soft brown sugar

5 preserving jars, 500 ml each, sterilized

Makes about 2.5 litres

Put all the ingredients into a heavy-based stainless steel or enamel saucepan. Bring to the boil. Stir, reduce the heat and simmer for 1 hour.

Pour into hot sterilized jars. Cover and seal. Label and date. Store for 4 weeks before using. After opening, keep covered in the refrigerator and use within 2 months.

Now you don't have to serve both mustard and horseradish sauce with the roast beef as this delicious variety combines both flavours. As a gift, fill several small decorative jars or pots and attach a small mustard spoon.

horseradish mustard

250 ml measured mustard powder, by volume, about 200 g

6 tablespoons horseradish. freshly grated or bottled

1 teaspoon sea salt

125 ml cider vinegar

1 tablespoon honey

4 tablespoons extra virgin olive oil

1 tablespoon freshly squeezed lemon juice

3 small preserving jars, about 125 ml each, sterilized

Makes about 300–375 ml

Put all the ingredients in a blender and process for 30 seconds or until the mixture is smooth and creamy.

Ladle into small attractive glass jars and seal tightly.

Store in the refrigerator for 1 week to 10 days before using, and eat within 3 months of opening. After opening, keep covered in the refrigerator and use within 1 month.

This mustard smells and tastes wonderful. It is quite spicy, but sweeter than most and it mellows with age. Once opened, mustard must be kept in the refrigerator and eaten within about a month.

sweet cardamom mustard

6 tablespoons mustard seeds

2 tablespoons mustard powder

1 teaspoon sea salt

½ teaspoon ground turmeric

10–12 cardamom pods

5–6 green peppercorns

1 teaspoon freshly grated nutmeg

4 tablespoons red wine

4 tablespoons cider vinegar

1 tablespoon honey

2 small preserving jars, about 125 ml each, sterilized

Makes about 250 ml

Coarsely grind the mustard seeds with a mortar and pestle or coffee grinder. Transfer to a bowl, then stir in the mustard powder, salt, turmeric and nutmeg.

Remove the seeds from the cardamom pods and crush with the peppercorns, using the back of a spoon, a rolling pin or a mortar and pestle. Add to the mustard and stir to blend the spices.

Stir in the wine, vinegar and honey until well blended and thick. If it is too thick add a little more wine or vinegar.

Cover the bowl and let stand for about 12 hours before spooning into small glass jars. Seal tightly and store for 3–4 weeks before using. After opening, keep covered in the refrigerator and use within 1 month.

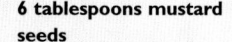

chutneys, relishes and mustards

Bouquet garni is the classic bundle of fresh, aromatic herbs used to flavour casseroles, soups and stock. The kitchen string makes it easier to remove after cooking – lots of flavour and no mess!

bouquet garni

1–2 fresh bay leaves	Your choice of:
sprigs of parsley	**7 cm piece of celery stalk**
sprigs of thyme	**sprigs of rosemary, lemon thyme, tarragon or other herbs**
	Makes 1 bouquet garni

Tie the herbs together with kitchen string, leaving a long loop of string to tie the bouquet to the handle of the pot – this makes it easier to remove from the finished dish. Alternatively, put the loose herbs in a double thickness of muslin. Secure tightly with string, leaving the string long as before.

Bouquet garni can be made from dried or powdered herbs, but they are no substitute for the fresh version.

Note: Fresh herbs, especially those with soft leaves, such as basil or parsley, wilt quickly. Assemble the bouquet just before presenting the gift.

A new and different bouquet garni – these traditional herbs from Thailand turn an ordinary dish into an extraordinary one. Compose at the last minute because coriander wilts quickly.

Thai-style bouquet garni

3 cm fresh ginger, sliced

a few sprigs of coriander

1 red chilli

Your choice of:

1 stalk of lemongrass

a sprig of kaffir lime leaves

sprigs of Thai mint or basil

Makes 1 bouquet garni

Put the ginger, coriander and chilli in a bundle, then add your choice of other ingredients. If using lemongrass, split it lengthways. Arrange all ingredients in a bundle and tie up with kitchen string. Use immediately.

index

Author's Acknowledgements

My special thanks to Elsa Petersen-Schepelern for her help and encouragement and to all the team at Ryland Peters & Small including designer, Sally Powell, Gabriella Le Grazie and Alison Starling, also to Rebecca Duke for her creative designing and ingenious packaging. To Clare Haynes and Sonia Brodie for their help with recipes and testing and to Janet Payne, Kay Partridge, Dimity Fairfax and to Pam Cooper for her fabulous friends. To my husband Michael Burton for putting up with kitchen chaos and most especially to Martin Brigdale for his generous hospitality and inspired photography.